T0209428

NATALIE EVE CUTSFORTH

S TAME YOUR ENERGY
Sensitivity

a **Tiger's Guide** to **Happiness**
for Sensitive People

BALBOA.PRESS
A DIVISION OF HAY HOUSE

Balboa Press books may be ordered through booksellers or by contacting:

Balboa Press
A Division of Hay House
1663 Liberty Drive
Bloomington, IN 47403
www.balboapress.com
1 (877) 407-4847

Print information available on the last page.

ISBN: 978-1-9822-4290-9 (sc)
ISBN: 978-1-9822-4289-3 (hc)
ISBN: 978-1-9822-4288-6 (e)

Library of Congress Control Number: 2020902472

Balboa Press rev. date: 02/17/2020

DEDICATION

This book is dedicated to all those who seek healing. To the human and animal souls that suffer when separated from their true nature. May you find peace.

ACKNOWLEDGMENTS

I bless with love . . .

My ancestors, angelic support, teachers, and clients for helping me understand my true nature and make peace with it. Thank you!

Those that encouraged me to write, from my grandmother, Florence Cutsforth, to my high school English teacher, Mr. Baldwin, to my fairy godmother, Lynne Burrows, fellow writers Jeff Taylor, Uncle Roger Paul, and the Summit Writers Group. Thank you!

Those who taught me determination, gave me courage and unconditional love—my mom, Patricia Stehle, my dad, Terry Cutsforth, and my spiritual mentor, Dawn Eagle Woman. Thank you!

The human and animal souls who taught me about healthy and unhealthy boundaries. Thank you!

My editor, Aleksandra Corwin, and intuitive assistant, Tracy Rubino—your enthusiasm and efficiency kept me on track. Thank you!

Tasha the tiger and the Wild Animal Sanctuary for inspiring me to write. Thank you!

CONTENTS

A TIGER'S TRUE NATURE

A tiger named Tasha was taken from her mother as a cub and kept in captivity in a faraway land. Her life was miserable. The unnatural climate and concrete floor of her cage were hard on her skin, the confinement limited her muscle use, and she was fed so little her ribs were visible through her fur. All she knew was suffering until one day the people at the Wild Animal Sanctuary rescued her from near death and moved her to a nature reserve built specifically to rehabilitate animals like her. As Tasha adjusted to her new environment, she had to learn a new way of being. A story in the Wild Animal Sanctuary's newsletter shared her caretaker's observation, that for Tasha, and many other misunderstood wildlife raised in captivity, "having to relearn trust is a life-altering experience." Her sensitive caretakers knew that true healing for Tasha would allow her to "open her heart wider than it has ever opened before."

Tasha's story is not so different from that of many energy sensitives. Energy sensitives, also known as empaths, often have navigated life not understanding their true nature. Empaths need to relearn how to trust their soul's guidance. Many have heard the whispers of their inner guidance but don't know how to translate it or what to do with the information. The messages from their body have long been disregarded, and they've often experienced intuitive hints as something "wrong" with them. Relearning trust for an empath means understanding that a knot in the stomach or anxiety for "no reason" is in fact an empathic sensitivity trying to get their attention

The seed of this confusion is usually planted when an empath is born in an environment that does not support their nature. Their soul suffers from malnourishment, no matter how loving their parents may have been. If the caretakers were not energy sensitives themselves or had been taught to "turn off" their sensitivity, they had no skills to pass along.

Life as an empath is a sacred journey requiring divine guidance. Having heightened energy sensitivity is simply a sign that you are not so far removed from the nature of wholeness each human is born with. All human beings hold the potential for that sacred connection, but today many are conditioned by society, or trauma, or a million other little imprints, to disregard the ability to receive information from the world by *sensing* it.

Like Tasha the tiger relearning the safety that comes with embracing her natural instincts, how can you relearn trust and open your heart as an empath? Is it really safe to open your heart wider than it has opened before? I believe it can be. But just as with Tasha, it won't happen as long as you are stuck in the old, confined place. It will require a transformation, one that involves movement and courage. You will have to feed your spirit a different type of nourishment than you have been, and learn a new way of holding your energy field so it can rest more deeply. Then trust for your inner guidance will emerge.

Unlike Tasha, you have free will. In this very moment you can choose to heal and break free of the limitations that you were born into. You have the power to align consciously with your soul's essence. If you do, you will discover why and how it is a good thing to be sensitive to energy. The most profound transformation and inner power can be yours when you relearn how to trust your inner guidance, open your heart, and embrace connection without absorbing the suffering of others.

REASONS EMPATHS DOUBT
THEIR INNER GUIDANCE

+ People telling you that what you sense is wrong.

+ The confusion created by feeling someone else's energy as if it is your own

+ It *sucks to feel so much* of the energy around you *all the time.*

Tasha the tiger was raised by humans, and the humans taught her to rely on them for survival. Her natural instincts were discouraged to tame her into submission. A predator powerful enough to kill her human keepers was raised in a way that made her forget the innate skills she had for survival. Among humans, there was no place for her wild nature.

One reason empaths learn not to trust or rely on their innate skills is because their insight makes the people around them uncomfortable. An empath might sense something that no one is talking about and say it, but have the people involved deny it. A child tells his mother, "Grandma is sad. I feel sad too." The mother, worried that her son feels sad and perhaps unwilling to be aware of her own mother's sadness, says reactively, "No, honey, she's not sad. See, she's smiling. Don't be sad." The child believes he's wrong for sensing this energy from his grandmother and begins to doubt or deny those empathic insights.

Over time, these seemingly small invalidations add up. Before too long the child is no longer clear that what he is sensing in those moments is actually *someone else's* energy. He learns not to freely speak these insights. He believes it must be him. He feels sad around a sad person and thinks, "*I must be sad.*" He doesn't have the awareness that he's absorbing someone else's sadness empathically.

Empaths read by feel. The first and most primal way of sensing the energy around you is through an energy field, and empaths feel it clearly right in their own bodies. If you haven't been taught that it is even possible to feel someone else's energy in your body, let alone how to have healthy energy boundaries, this can be a very confusing experience. Is it me feeling this or is it you? How do I know?

Because of this, empaths can be more easily swayed by the desires of people around them to make choices that aren't aligned with their own truth. You feel the energy of the person whose truth it is and misunderstand it as your own. A person is attracted to you. You feel their sexual energy and think it's yours. You say yes to a date, then walk away and realize once out of their energy field that you aren't at all attracted to the person.

The energy of others has a stronger influence on the empath than on the average person. This is particularly true of negative energy, because people ooze anger, depression, and fear rather than keeping it contained in their aura. It creates a toxic cloud wherever they are, and the empath in their presence takes on the poison and suffers.

You might have coffee with a friend who is in emotional pain, listen compassionately with a desire to help, all the while taking on a lot of their pain. As an empath, it gets into your space because you are openly feeling into their energy to read it. The friend feels better after the conversation, not just because they got to share their experiences, but because they were able to dump a lot of their pain. They received a healing from you.

A key to finding peace as an empath is learning to have empathy without absorbing the pain of the wounded. Taking on someone's suffering to help them heal results in you needing to heal yourself. It drags you down to match their pain. Over time you'll be so exhausted, you won't be able to lift people up out of their pain anymore.

The fundamental truth, and something that all empaths need to understand, is that you can help a person heal without taking on their suffering. This is surprising to a lot of empaths who feel responsible for taking on the pain and suffering of people they care about.

> **Energy Shift Tip:** Visualize offering the person in need grounding. Imagine a tree rooted beside their body available to stabilize them. This way they can choose to receive it or not. Then send them a gold bubble of healing energy, rather than bringing their pain into your energy field to heal it. (Details in the Step-by-Step Guide)

Your healing nature as an empath can be so deeply unconscious that you see what needs healing in another and try to fix or heal a person who hasn't asked for it. If the person hasn't asked you for a healing, they can feel violated by you *reading* their pain and bringing attention to it.

They may even send you an energy whack to create a boundary, which is another confusing message for empaths. Have you ever thought you were helping someone but found they were angry instead of grateful? In all innocence, most empaths don't know they are violating someone's boundaries by reading them without permission. How would you know if no one taught you?

Most of all, many empaths don't trust their inner guidance because it sucks to feel so much. An energy sensitive often believes that if they embrace their intuitive nature, they will only feel worse. This is deeply programmed from all of the overwhelming and confusing experiences most empaths grow up with. Empaths are told they feel "too much"; their insights are often ignored and invalidated, so the default way to cope is to shut that part of themselves down.

As a child, I vividly remember sitting in church with my mom and feeling unsafe. We went to church regularly, and most of the time I felt fine. But that day there was a guest speaker. Although we never had personal contact, I remember exactly where I was sitting—in the middle, near the back of the room—and that my stomach felt queasy, and my female parts were disturbed by his sexual energy. At that age, I didn't know what I was experiencing, nor did I say anything to my mom about it. I never saw him again. I just felt icky. Now that I know my empathic signals better, I'm aware that his sexual energy had no boundaries, and it felt like a violation because I was reading the energy.

As a young empath I experienced being around someone depressed or angry and found myself feeling depressed or angry. After walking away from that person, I felt like myself again, sometimes within moments. Other times it took hours. Ultimately, what got me started on the path of clairvoyant training was a desire to turn off the constant uncontrollable experience of feeling so much.

HOW EMPATHS RELEARN TRUST

✦ Develop healthy boundaries with energy.

✦ Leave draining environments.

✦ Nurture your spiritual and empathic needs.

✦ Learn the language of your inner guidance.

For Tasha the tiger, relearning trust started with having her basic needs taken care of. She had more space, an environment that didn't agitate her skin, food that nourished her body. Over time, her new caretakers at the sanctuary used the language she spoke—physical posturing—and respect of her boundaries to show her they trusted her. She began to believe she could trust them too. Now her eyes are brighter and her coat healthier, and she's beginning to act like the powerful tiger she is.

As an empath, you too have to start the healing process with more space. You do this by setting clear energy boundaries for yourself. Having boundaries keeps others from getting in your energy field, and prevents you from merging into theirs. To do this takes a regular practice of defining your aura bubble, and clearing other people's energy out of your energy field. You can also put grace-filled protection around your energy field. (How to protect your energy is detailed in the Step-by-Step Guide).

Space gives you better perspective and ability to notice the parts of your environment that are agitating your energy. It allows you to recognize certain situations or people in your life that drain you. With room for yourself, you can see what relationships are out of balance, or when someone is chronically taking more than they are offering and dumping their negative energy on you, so they feel better and you feel worse.

Your relationships may need to change or be updated to honor your growth. Or they may need to fade away if they aren't a fit.

Most of all, nourishing your empathic self is essential to getting out of *empath survival mode.* This is a state of chronic energetic stress where you live with anxiety or check out of your body so you don't have to feel it. When your fuel tank is on empty, your vehicle is going nowhere.

> **Energy Shift Tip:** Reset your grounding cord to *get in your body* if you feel checked out. Put your bare feet on the Earth. Be the tree and the roots supported by Earth, branches reaching to the sunlight. (Details in the Step-by-Step Guide)

After giving yourself space, you have a chance to reclaim the energy that is required to engage with trust. You must first learn to trust that you will not be short on the fuel needed to survive. You'll know you won't be lacking because you will have learned how to generate energy yourself. You'll make choices that nourish your sensitive nature and refill your spirit from chronic depletion.

There is no pill you can take to alter this aspect of your nature in a way that brings peace. Gaining knowledge helps, but the true solution is consistent, focused practice in setting your energy field, until having healthy energy boundaries becomes second nature. You must set aside intentional time to clear out energetic clutter in your body and your surroundings. Breathe deeply. Visualize and define your personal energetic space. Let yourself feel *you* without others altering the way you feel.

Visualization is a powerful tool for energy sensitives. You can use it to set your energy field, ground your body, protect your aura, and fill in with energy from the earth and cosmos. When you call your energy back to yourself with visualization, you reclaim it from where it was scattered or left behind. I'll show you how in the Step-by-Step Guide section.

Through all of this, you are building a trusted relationship with your inner guidance. You are learning the new language that lets you hear how intuition communicates with you. This moves your empathic radar out of survival mode. Instead of reading by feeling everything in your environment, you will learn to read by seeing intuitively, and move into thrive mode. When you learn to *see*, you don't end up taking on or absorbing what you empathically *feel*. To *see* is to access intuitive information through your third eye, in the center of your head, rather than leaving your energy field open and reading by feeling it in your body.

Energy Shift Tip: Visualize taking an elevator up from the place just below your belly button—where you read by feeling the energy around you—to your third eye (center of head), where you can see the energy without it altering the way you feel.

CREATE A SANCTUARY FOR YOUR SENSES

- Get clear on what is yours versus what comes from someone else.
- Let go of a feeling of responsibility to heal others.
- Learn what it means to have equal exchanges of energy.
- Discern when your way of reading energy disturbs others.

Tasha had never met another tiger. The energy of her own kind—hearing them, smelling them, and seeing them—threatened her sense of safety and overwhelmed her senses. Fortunately, her caretakers gave Tasha a slow introduction to the other tigers, first moving her to a large enclosure nearby the main tiger enclosure, where a dozen other tigers resided. Once she was used to their sounds and smell, the staff removed a small area of visual barricade on the adjoining fence so she could look through it if she desired. Tasha didn't have to see the other tigers all the time but could slowly get used to their presence.

As a human empath, you must take a few more important steps to find your inner sanctuary too. One is learning the difference between what is your energy and what is someone else's energy—for many empaths this is a fundamentally confusing element of existence. The other step vital to bringing you back into balance is letting go of feeling responsible for healing other people simply because you see their suffering. These two draining habits are often intertwined. Give yourself the grace Tasha received, taking it slow as you explore your new energy boundaries.

As I mentioned earlier, when you are an empath, it is easy to confuse what *you* feel with what you are feeling *from others*. Another person's energy can overwhelm your empathic senses and throw you off balance, it can create the sensation that you are unsafe, or that you are the one feeling fear, anger, depression, and so forth, when it is really someone else's energy you are picking up on. This is because those strong emotions in people around you alter your energy field, confusing your physical, mental, and emotional radar.

It takes time to learn the subtleties of what you are sensing. Like Tasha learning the smells and sounds of other tigers before seeing them, visualization and practice changing energetic boundaries helps. But even with skills and practice, you are constantly encountering new energetic exchanges with people that may test your boundaries. Even when you are well versed in setting clear intentions that define what you will allow or disallow, you can still encounter people who will try to get into your space through trickier methods.

When you need clarity about the source of uncomfortable energy you sense, ask yourself these three questions. The answer will help you know what to do next. To find the answer, close your eyes, and imagine a rose directly in front of you. Ask the rose to move right, then to move left. Ask which direction is your *yes* and which is your *no*. Then ask each of these questions, and notice which direction the rose goes:

1) Is it *me*? Do I feel this way? Is it an awareness of my own physical, mental, or emotional state?

2) Is it *someone else*? Am I tuned in to someone in my life who is feeling this way? Did someone I live with, work with, or interact with alter my energy?

3) Is it *something else*? Is there a harmful attachment or spirit altering my experience or feeding off of my energy? (Note: primary ways empaths take on a harmful attachment are healing another person, or as the result of a trauma, or as part of a family agreement, or by opening your energy field with mind-altering substances.)

If it is you, allow the energy to move. Walk. Write. Cry. Laugh. Scream into a pillow. Take a bath. Let it out. The only path of relief is to move through it.

*If it is **someone else**,* notice if you feel it in a certain physical spot—visualize their energy moving out of your body and your aura field. See their energy go into a bubble and float back to them. Then pop the bubble over their head. If it is negative energy, you may choose to send the bubble to a faraway place and pop it so it is not being returned to the person.

*If it is **something else**—*a harmful attachment, a soul without a body that is in your space—know that you can tell it to leave, and end your agreement to be its host. Visualize connecting it with a gold cord to the Source of all energy (Supreme Being, God/Goddess, Higher Power), and move it out of your space up to Source energy. This allows the soul to receive a healing and take its next step.

Then visualize the soul contract that allowed this soul without a body to attach to you. Cross out the signatures and burn the contract to confirm it is ended. Then ask your soul record keeper to update your soul records (akashic records) with this information. Send the same update to the akashic record keeper of the soul you ended the contract with.

Energy Shift Tip: Whenever you move negative or harmful energy out of your space, it is helpful to put protection roses around your aura bubble in six directions—in front, behind, right, left, above, and below. (Details in the Step-by-Step Guide) Watch this video to help: https://www.nataliecutsforth.com/freebies/steps-to-set-and-protect-your-energy/

The step of sending someone's energy out of your space and back to them might feel uncomfortable at first. Most people are conditioned to feel responsible to match another person's emotions as a show of compassion. Because empaths can feel these unspoken energies as if they are their own (e.g., you feel *their* suffering in *your* heart), the assumption is you need to do something, right? Not necessarily.

Just because you sense someone's suffering doesn't mean it is helpful to them when you take it away or take it on yourself. They are in their own growth process, and taking it away may extend the suffering or the lesson they are working on in their soul path. Plus, you may have energetic consequences from taking on something that wasn't yours; physical symptoms such as weakened immune system, weight gain, or energy loss are not uncommon results.

That is not to say that there aren't completely appropriate places and times to offer healing. I am an intuitive healer. Healers are needed on the planet. But the important distinction to understand here is that empaths often feel they *have to give and give and give*, because there is so much pain everywhere.

Unless you have balanced exchanges of energy, you do yourself and others a disservice. There are times when people with more energy, skills, and resources *do* need to extend help to those in need. Tasha's caretakers did this when they rescued her from a dire situation and near death. You can receive a lot from giving this way. But healing others as an automatic reaction to feeling their pain is often not an appropriate or healthy response for the giver or receiver. Healing does not last, transform, and uplift the good of all if it is not part of an agreed-upon and healthy energy exchange. This is why it is so critical to discern when you have permission from the person to provide healing, and to offer it only with that agreement.

In your day-to-day relationships, you are always exchanging energy, giving and receiving. Empaths chronically overextend themselves by absorbing energy or healing others, often when it hasn't been requested. Over-giving causes an energy deficit in yourself. Taking more than you give contributes to an energy deficit in others.

As you relearn trust, part of the journey is trusting that others are on their own soul path. Allowing them to experience their lessons or karma (positive and negative) without stepping in to take it away is an important part of the contribution you can make to the energy balance that keeps the universe in motion. Trust that having open communication about energy exchange will lead to more balance and health in your relationships, and all energy on the planet.

Your job as an empath is to understand what you are experiencing and set healthy boundaries.

It gets easier when you realize that absorbing energy from someone is not the same as healing the person. Your body can absorb arsenic dissolved in water by drinking the water, but this does not heal or purify the water. You've moved the arsenic from the form it was in, and now have it in your body, but the toxin has not gone away. The toxin has simply now changed *your* body in the material sense, and this is what is happening with empaths in the energetic sense.

Healers, on the other hand, remove the negative energy from another person. Without boundaries and certain skills, healers may absorb it and find themselves toxified by it. Many professional healers get burnt out, and become emotionally distant or ill from *absorbing* the energy rather than helping the person move it and transmute it. With energy-conscious skills, healers can help people in pain without the risk of taking it on themselves.

While professional healers operate with an open acknowledgment of their energy exchange agreement, empaths often have unconscious or hidden energy exchange agreements. These can lead to resentment of those who take your energy.

That is why anger, irritation, or resentment are neon lights pointing to the reset button for your energy boundaries. Is someone violating them? Is your lack of boundaries letting others get in your space? Are you getting in someone else's space by not honoring their boundaries?

> **Energy Shift Tip:** Reset your boundaries, visualize your aura bubble as perfectly balanced around your body, about fingertip distance away with your arms outstretched. Paint it a color to define where your energy field ends and where others begin.

To create your sanctuary means taking responsibility, not just for how you're affected by others' energy but also for how your energy affects others. Energy sensitives have the habit of getting in another person's head to see how they are doing, often because they want to know what to expect. In order to feel safe, they "read" a person psychically, whenever they can. Some empaths grow up thinking this is normal because they come from a family with no boundaries.

Whatever the why, know this: your inner peace depends on only reading people with permission.

When you read someone without their permission, they feel it. Sometimes they will send you an energy whack to make you back off. If they have a similar lack of boundaries, they may be fine with it or even expect you to know things they haven't told you. Regardless, tracking someone else this way will muddy your clarity, will drain your energy, and can make you feel crazy because you are getting information that is not meant for you.

It can feel scary to let go of reading people this way if you've relied on it for your personal safety. But reading others to determine what they need before they ask, or to protect yourself, is the leading cause of stress, anxiety, and exhaustion in empaths. Being psychically "on" all the time burns out your adrenal gland. Your body translates it as the fight-or-flight stress response. This keeps your body's resources mobilized to deal with a threat that may or may not be relevant to you, simply because you are reading another person or many other people at once.

Adjusting the way you read, to only read when you have permission, means you are just looking at your information. You still get the inner guidance you need to ensure your safety relative to others. Plus, you get the inner peace that comes with being responsible for your experience and not responsible for what you can see of another's experiences.

Your energy sensitivity serves you best when you can clearly see a person lying to you, or know you are safe, or discern your next step. It doesn't serve you when you get in someone else's head to try to see what they see. Your gift is to have information *for you*.

Energy Shift Tip: If you sense your energy is in someone's space, pull your attention back into the center of your head, your third eye. Then point it to your higher self for guidance. You do this by closing your eyes and focusing your gaze on the point just above your head.

STEP-BY-STEP GUIDE TO RECLAIM YOUR ENERGY

✦ Define your personal space.

✦ Amp up your energy level.

✦ Set protection for your energy field.

✦ Focus your attention on your inner guidance.

✦ Strengthen and rebalance your energy.

Living with empathic sensitivity requires maintenance of your energy field. These simple yet powerful practices are where to begin. Once this energetic foundation becomes second nature, so much more is possible.

1) Define Your Personal Space:

Start with your personal space, and define energetically where your energy field ends and begins. This is key to feeling good. Here's how you do it:

Close your eyes and take a deep breath.

Notice the tip of your tailbone.

Imagine it has a line of energy extending from it, all the way down into the center of the Earth. This is your grounding cord. It is fun to see it as a tree trunk, animal tail, beam of light, or marble column. See the cord plug in or grow roots connecting you to the source of energy in the planet. Your grounding cord is your energetic foundation. It is flexible and also helps your spirit stay in your body.

Now see a bubble around your whole body. Imagine your arms are stretched out wide to embrace all of the love in the universe. Your aura bubble begins at the tips of your fingers on your open arms. Give the bubble a color that evokes the energy you would like to feel—peaceful, energized, creative . . . you decide. Tuck it into your grounding cord so there are no holes or gaps. Your aura bubble is your energetic sanctuary. It sends a clear message to others about your personal space.

Bring your attention to the center of your head, to your third eye, the place between your ears and behind your eyes. Clear out your psychic space by imagining a hose or fan blowing it clean of what is not yours or not in present time. This removes any outdated thoughts or other people's energy that is in your head so you can see your own information, free of any influences. Now you are ready for Step 2.

2) Amp Up Your Energy Level:

See a golden orb above your head. It is magnetic, and you can call your energy back to you from anywhere you have left it . . . with a person, in a place, in an unresolved experience, or out in the future. Intend that all of these bits and pieces of your soul's essence come back to this golden ball. If you like, imagine infusing this golden orb with a vibration you would like to feel more of, such as ease, playfulness, prosperity, clarity, and so forth. Then pop the golden orb and watch it flow down into the top of your head like honey, filling up every cell of your body—your head, neck, shoulders, arms, fingertips . . . your heart, belly, hips, legs—all the way down to the tips of your toes. Extend the energy in all directions until it fills up your aura bubble.

Now you are grounded, in your personal bubble; your intuitive space is clear, and you have filled in with your own energy. It's time for Step 3.

3) Set Protection for Your Energy Field:

Visualize a beautiful red rose in front of you, just outside of your aura bubble. The blossom is open and as wide as your shoulders. This rose is set at a high vibrational frequency of protection that does not block you from receiving. It has a long stem that is grounded down into the earth. In your mind's eye, replicate the rose in six directions on the outside of your aura bubble—to your right, to your left, in front of you, behind you, above your head, and below your feet. Your protection roses filter out negative or unwanted energy you encounter that may try to get into your energy sanctuary.

When you are looking to align with your soul path or would like to ask for answers from your guidance, take Step 4.

4) Focus Your Attention on Your Inner Guidance:

Notice your attention is out in front of you. It might be focused on another person, a task, or even something in the past that feels unresolved. See your attention like a long fishing line at the end of a fishing pole pointed in the direction of your focus. And now imagine reeling in that line, until all of the energy is back in the center of your head, your third eye. Then direct your attention by focusing that energy with your inner gaze straight up toward your crown, the top of your head—this is where your personal guidance gets dropped in from your higher self and the divine. Sit with this sensation and notice how it relaxes your whole body.

Now is a good time to ask your soul self that question or simply sit open to information.

If you would like to take more time to clean out your energetic body, balance your chakras, and fill up with good energy, there are a few more steps to nurture your empath sanctuary.

5) Strengthen and Rebalance Your Energy:

Planet Earth and the cosmos have energy available to you. This energy will both clean out and revitalize your energy body.

Sit with both feet flat on the floor. Reach with your mind's eye down into the center of the Earth. See its energy as a green current of light begin to come up into the soles of your feet and legs, through your knees and hips, into your root chakra at the base of your spine. Intend that some of that Earth energy is sent back down your grounding cord to recirculate.

Now reach with your mind's eye up into the stars. See the cosmic energy as a golden current of light coming down into the top of your head and down your back in two or four channels on both sides of your spine. Notice the energy meet up with the Earth energy in your root chakra. Send a little bit of the cosmic energy down your grounding cord and watch the rest mix, swirling the green and golden light of Earth and Cosmic energy. See this powerful healing energy go up the front of your body in two channels, one on each side of your chakras. The Earth and Cosmic energies pass each chakra at the three o'clock and nine o'clock positions; each chakra spins, is cleaned out, and is rebalanced. When the energy channels pass your shoulders, send a bit of the energy down your arms—they are your creative channels—and out the palms of your hands. Watch the rest continue up and fountain out the top of your head.

You are filling up with energy while receiving an energy cleanout from both Earth and Cosmos.

Note What Works for You

My favorite grounding cord image is a . . .

possibilities: tree trunk, beam of light, animal tail, or one of your own imagination

_____

_____

_____

_____

_____

_____

The colors that feel good on my aura bubble are . . .

_____

_____

_____

_____

_____

_____

_____

The tool for clearing out my third eye that works best for me is a . . .

possibilities: fan, hose, bouncer, rose or one of your own imagination

_____

_____

_____

_____

I feel best when I fill-in with these three vibrations

possibilities: clarity, prosperity, playfulness, courage, grace, inspiration, efficiency, strength, love, peace, radiant beauty

1 _____

2 _____

3 _____

The most empowering color for my protection rose is . . .

_____

_____

_____

_____

Connect with Your Inner Guidance

I request guidance from my higher self on . . .

possibilities: ask a specific question, ask your spirit to show you what your soul needs to know at this time, ask for direction in areas of your life such as relationship, career, home, finances, health

WHY IT'S A GIFT TO BE AN EMPATH

Being an energy sensitive doesn't have to be hard or difficult. Your energy sensitivity is part of your soul's purpose in this life. It is an ability that you can gain skill in, and when you use it with consistency, you will feel the benefits of this aspect of your nature.

There are many benefits of being energy sensitive. Number one is personal safety. If you sense a person's energy is unsafe, you can do something about it. Sensing the energy around you can help you make better choices if you trust it.

Every empath I know has a story where they wish they would have listened to their intuition but disregarded it and regretted the consequences. They didn't trust a person but said yes anyway and were taken advantage of.

Or they did trust their inner guidance not knowing why and found out later. For example, they felt compelled to linger when late to an appointment and missed getting into a ten-car pileup by minutes.

Another benefit, when you empathically sense others' needs but simultaneously have good boundaries, is that it helps create more fulfilling intimate connections. People feel safe with you because they sense you honor their space. They don't have to create the boundary for you or withdraw to feel more comfortable. It also means you feel safer energetically, allowing you to open your heart to deeper connection.

Empaths have inherent intuitive ability. While anyone can learn to access their intuition, empaths are highly intuitive and just need to remove the doubts created by early life suppression and learn how to translate the information into something their human minds can understand.

The most valuable gift of being an empath is access to your own guidance. It may have felt hard or confusing for you to access the guidance up to now because it was blurred by others' energy. Once you learn how to set boundaries for your energy field, move other people out of your space, and stop absorbing everything around you, your guidance becomes much clearer.

Empaths are more tapped in than most people to that sixth sense but often feel drained and tapped out from sensing so much. Learning to trust your sixth sense is a life-altering experience allowing you to live your true nature.

TRUST IS A LIFE-ALTERING EXPERIENCE

Tasha can't go back into the wild and experience life as a free tiger. She doesn't have the skills to survive, nor the awareness that her experience is not normal. But she's learning new skills now at the sanctuary. She's learning trust. Trusting her senses may allow her one day to share her space with other tigers for the first time. Equally important, she's healing the wounds from years of being separated from her true nature. Her body feels better, she has more space, and her existence is no longer energy depleting.

Like Tasha, you can't go back to what life would have been like before all the experiences that led up to this moment, but you can create an inner sanctuary as an empath and learn new skills. You can learn to feel better in your body and build trust with your energy sensitivity. You can heal the wounds created by years of invalidation and absorbing the energy around you.

Like Tasha, your path to healing may also require healers who can see what you don't see in yourself and nurture you through the process. Maybe you have been on the path of healing for some time, and question why you still struggle after working through mental and emotional wounds? It is because as an empath, your healing process also requires clearing the energy associated with the experiences.

That may include cutting energy cords from other people. You may need to erase beliefs that were created by those who invalidated your energy sensitivity. Your healing may require release of unconscious programs that have you compelled to read others even at the expense of yourself. Whatever your experience has been, know that you can change these patterns and reclaim your inner peace.

One of the key areas of healing is the relationship between your body and spirit. Empaths spend more time with their spirit out of their body than most people. It feels safer to *not*

TAME YOUR ENERGY SENSITIVITY

feel so much of what the body is sensing. Here are some signs that your spirit is not fully in your body: you have difficulty sleeping, bump into things, lack a sense of heartfelt passion for things that used to light you up in a positive way.

Your healing starts with awareness of energy and setting healthy boundaries. It continues with inviting your spirit to spend more time in your body. You do that by calling it into your crown chakra from where it is lingering, just above your head. Ask your soul to come all the way down into your fingers and toes. The more you are *in* your body the greater your ability to keep other people or things out of your space.

Once in your body with energy boundaries, you can use energy tools to heal old patterns that keep past wounds alive. Energy tools are a way to focus your sixth sense to actively participate in sensations you experience. You use visualization with the third eye to transform one state of energy to another state of energy. Moving energy is the path to self-healing for sensitive people.

Energy Shift Tip: When you feel blocked or stuck, take a few breathes and notice where you feel it in your body. Identify what chakra that relates to, (see glossary) to better understand what is blocked. Now visualize a rose that is sticky and imagine that rose cleaning out your blocked chakra. Once all the gunk is gathered up in the rose, toss the rose up into the stars to dissolve.

Trusting your senses and feeling safe in your body is your path to happiness as an empath. As you heal and apply the skills to create your empathic sanctuary, you will find yourself, like Tasha, able to "open your heart wider than it has ever opened before" a life-altering experience.

Heal Your Energy

Use the following questions and answers to identify areas that are ready for healing through movement of energy.

After you identify each energy limitation use your third eye to visualize moving the energy out of your energy field into a bubble. Then send the energy bubble to a faraway place to recycle in the sea of infinite energy with no harm done. If you identify a cord or hook, cut the cord and connect it to source energy (god/goddess, supreme being, your higher power). This gives it another source of energy so it does not try to reconnect to you immediately.

Do I notice when my spirit isn't fully in my body? What are the signs that I'm not in my body?

_____

_____

_____

_____

_____

_____

What areas do I feel blocked or limited by my sensitivity? Where do I feel it in my body What chakra is this (see glossary)?

_____

_____

_____

_____

_____

_____

_____

What outdated beliefs or pictures (way of seeing things) am I ready to let go of?

_____

_____

_____

_____

_____

_____

_____

Are there energy cords or hooks from another person or people attached to me? Where are they attached to my body? What charka is this (see glossary)?

_____

_____

_____

_____

_____

_____

_____

_____

_____

_____

_____

_____

_____

_____

_____

_____

HOW TO BE A HEALTHY, HAPPY EMPATH

In summary, here are the essential areas of awareness to consider as you work to create your empath energy sanctuary:

1. It's time to validate your sixth sense and choose people in your life that do.

2. Healthy energy boundaries can be learned and exercised like any fitness regimen.

3. When you feel depleted, you can reclaim your energy and fill your own cup by using guided visualization, the first three steps in the Step-by-Step Guide to Reclaim Your Energy.

4. You don't have to heal others just because you sense their suffering. By taking on their pain, you may be

enabling them to stay stuck in a lesson longer than they would have otherwise been.

5. If you are struggling to get clear about what you sense, start with asking the three questions: Is it me? Is it someone else? Is it something else? The answer will help you know what to do next.

6. You can protect yourself from draining, negative, or harmful energy.

7. It doesn't have to feel bad to be highly sensitive. It can be fun.

8. With safe space, Tasha the tiger is learning to trust her true nature—so can you.

Use these steps daily to maintain healthy energy boundaries and your empathic clarity:

1. Define your personal space – Aura bubble, grounding cord, and clear center of head.

2. Fill up with good energy – Call your energy back to you and fill up with it.

3. Set protection – See roses in six directions as a graceful filter to others' energy.

4. Adjust your attention – Align your focus to your inner guidance.

5. Strengthen and rebalance – Earth and Cosmic energy cleanout and chakra balance.

For more information, please check out the resources available for free on my website at http://www. nataliecutsforth.com.

EPILOGUE

Tasha continues her journey to discover her true nature and connect with her kind in the care of the Wild Animal Sanctuary in Keenesburg, Colorado. A portion of the proceeds of this book are donated to sponsor her care. Visit her and over five hundred rescued lions, tigers, jaguars, bears, and wolves, or support them with a donation at https://www.wildanimalsanctuary.org/.

GLOSSARY

Akashic records: A storehouse of all that has occurred in the universe. The soul's memories conscious or unconscious, also called the Book of Life. For the individual it refers to a soul's experiences across lifetimes.

Aura: The energetic field around a body containing a person's soul essence. A bubble of energy radiating from the body, approximately three feet in every direction.

Chakra: Seven energy centers in the human body. A map an empath can use to read, understand, and manage energy in the body. Each chakra has a specific role to hold and move energy. Here's a brief description of each chakra.

Root chakra, at the base of the spine, holds the energy of food, shelter and survival.

Sacral chakra, below the belly button, holds the energy of creation, sexuality and empathic feeling.

Solar plexus chakra, above the belly button, holds one's will, power and capacity to bring creations into a physical form.

Heart chakra, holds the energy of love for others and Self, as well as one's true essence.

Throat chakra, is the center of communication, expression and taking in information.

Third eye chakra, center of head behind the physical eyes, holds analytical thought, intuitive sight and the capacity for neutrality.

Crown chakra, at the top of the head, is where one connects with source and accesses information from their guidance.

Empath or sensitive person: A person who psychically reads energy, often feeling it in their body, whether positive or painful. Their senses are altered by the energy of people they come in contact with. A sensitive person in this context is not defined as the person expressing extreme emotions, rather their sensitivity is to the energy and emotions of people around them.

Energy: A frequency some people can sense, a sixth sense that is not measured with sight, sound, taste, touch or smell. Energy between people is always in motion. When in balance, it's given and received equally. When out of balance, energy is sucked from or dumped on a person.

Intuition: Awareness of information from non-material sources such as energy. Intuition is the sixth sense that reads information beyond sight, sound, taste, touch, or smell. It provides inner guidance in response to life experiences.

Karma: The energetic ledger of past actions for a soul in this life and other lifetimes. Karma is neither bad or good, it is simply the balance or imbalance of exchanges of energy.

Read: To have intuition about a person, to psychically see information about them.

See: To acquire information from the sixth sense rather that what is known with the analytical mind. It also refers to visualizing movement of energy with your third eye.

Sixth Sense: To see or read energy.

Transformation: A soul's process of growth. Releasing what no longer serves you to make room for new experiences. A lifelong process that includes clearing karma, updating soul contracts, aligning with one's purpose, staying curious and trusting your inner guidance.

Whack: A negative energetic hit that often accompanies verbal or written exchange.

ABOUT THE AUTHOR

Natalie Cutsforth is an intuitive healer and teacher offering life-changing transformation through private sessions, courses, and retreats with clients all over the world. Her spiritual training began in 1997 with a powerful dream that led to more than a decade of intensive work with spiritual mentor Dawn Eagle Woman. In 2000 she began to explore her psychic ability at the Inner Connection Institute in Denver, Colorado, receiving her Clairvoyant certification.

After a decade of her own healing, study, and practice, she began to see clients, combining the principles from her education with her unique capacity to see and heal. She helps clients heal their soul memory (akashic records), remove energy blocks, clear harmful attachments, and update their soul contracts—the agreements made before entering this body or while in it with yourself or other souls. She teaches empaths how to understand what they are reading and set boundaries to gracefully navigate sensitivity.

Natalie was influenced early in life by the freedom and work ethic of her family's hippie ranch in the coastal mountains of Oregon. Today she has created her own sanctuary, a twenty-acre homestead in central Oregon, where she grows organic food and is restoring the land.

A graduate of University of Colorado Boulder, Bachelor of Arts International Affairs program, Natalie spent twenty-two years living in Denver and working in the geographic information systems industry. She is blessed to be doing her soul work full-time seeing clients, writing, and teaching. And enjoys the balance of using both analytical and intuitive skills to create a magical life.

Join Natalie's Empath Strength Training practice group to continue reclaiming your power. https://www.nataliecutsforth. com/work-with-me/empath-strength-training-membership/

Printed in the United States
By Bookmasters